STEAM'S LAMENT

4-6-0s on the Southern Region

Kevin Derrick

Strathwood

STEAM'S LAMENT
4-6-0s on the Southern Region

First published 2022
ISBN 978-1-913390-26-6

All rights reserved. No part of this book may be reproduced or transmitted in any form or by any means, electronic or mechanical, including photocopying, recording or by any information storage and retrieval system, without written permission from the Publisher in writing.

Copyright Strathwood Publishing 2022
4 Shuttleworth Road,
Elm Farm Industrial Estate,
Bedford MK41 0EP
Telephone number 01234 328792
www.strathwood.co.uk

Above: Maunsell's Class N15X 32330 Cudworth stands in the lines awaiting a return to work alongside the works at Eastleigh after a minor repair around September 1949. *Strathwood Library Collection*

Contents

	Page
The Stuff of Legends	4
Maunsell's Sea Dogs	78
Lest We Forget	98
Paddleboxes	110
Chonkers	115
Urie's S15s	138
Maunsell's S15s	154
More 4-6-0s on the Southern	178

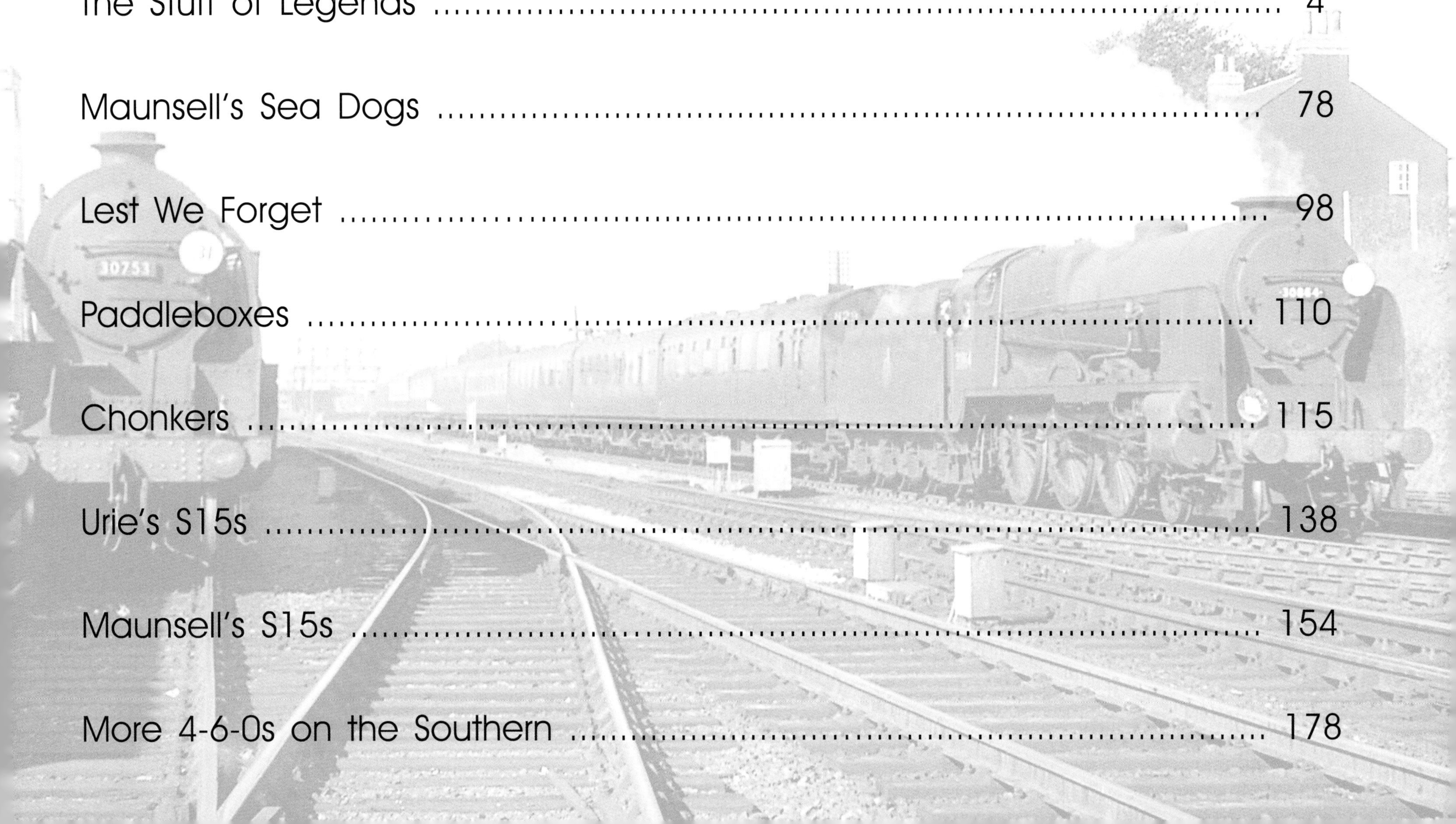

The Stuff of Legends

As a Salisbury allocated locomotive the appearance of 30448 Sir Tristram here at Exmouth Junction would have been commonplace through the 1950s. This view is post May 1955 as she is now paired with the ex-Class H15 tender from 30478 which would see it through to withdrawal on 29 August 1960. *The Transport Treasury*

Opposite: Unfortunately for 30449 Sir Torre scrapping came just before the start of the sixties during the week ending 26 December 1959 at Eastleigh Works, just a week after being declared as withdrawn. Here she is at Nine Elms complete with her water cart tender on 8 September 1956 visiting from Salisbury. *Colour Rail*

This would be one of the very last duties for 30450 Sir Kay as it heads up the bank out of Waterloo into Vauxhall on 21 August 1960, as it would posted as withdrawn thirteen days later, and scrapped completely within a month of this shot. At this time, the scrappers at Eastleigh Works were being kept busy week in, week out. But time would come for 30451 Sir Lamorak as well before too much longer. Here she is drawing into Woking with an up service on 28 April 1962. Time would be called a few weeks later on 16 June and all trace would be gone by the end of the same month.
Photos: Colour Rail & James Harrold/The Transport Library

Opposite: Another of the Salisbury fleet to go before the 1960s would be 30452 Sir Meliagrance when taken out of use on 22 August 1959 and dumped at Eastleigh to await her fate with the cutters. Here she is engaged on the 08:46 Salisbury to Waterloo semi-fast making the stop at Basingstoke on 13 June in her final summer. *Colour Rail*

Below: Two young lads watch as it is action stations before departure from Salisbury with this up express for Waterloo on 17 August 1957. There may have been false hopes of saving her when withdrawn on 8 July 1961 at Eastleigh Works as she was set aside until the week ending 21 October 1961. *R.O. Tuck/Rail Archive Stephenson*

Opposite: Those eight-wheel water cart tenders may look old fashioned, but 30454 Queen Guinevere still cuts a fine sight running under a clean exhaust past Bramshott Woods on 17 February 1957, her reign would come to an end during October the following year with Eastleigh disposing of her remains the month after. *Trevor Owen/Colour Rail*

Below: It would be a familiar tale for the bold Sir Lancelot 30455, by being sent to Eastleigh Works in April 1959 and rapidly cut up within just a few weeks. No signs of what was to come when seen setting out from Woking bound for Bournemouth on 31 July 1954 during its spell as a 70A Nine Elms engine. *Peter Pescod/The Transport Treasury*

A chance to play spot the difference with not only livery, tenders but also boilers as we see 30456 Sir Galahad resplendent in malachite green at Andover Junction in June 1949, against her portrait taken at Basingstoke with what looks like a fresh load of slack in her tender on 21 June 1959.
Photos: Strathwood Library Collection & K.L. Cook/Rail Archive Stephenson

In steam days the approaches to Vauxhall station from the Waterloo end were popular for many a cameraman and spotter to enjoy the sights and sounds of London departures such as this one headed by 30457 Sir Bedivere in September 1958. There were a number of differences within the batches of Class N15 King Arthurs as we will see covering the whole of the class. Numbers 30448-30452 were all built during 1925 to the former LSWR loading gauge and based upon the original design by Urie, thus precluding them for work away from the Western Section. Whereas 30453-30457 were built under Maunsell with the first one built lending its name to the entire class as King Arthurs. *Colour Rail*

Numbers 30736-30755 were Urie's original Class N15 locomotives built between 1918-1923 with substantial eight-wheel bogie tenders. Dressed in a hybrid Malachite livery complete with sunshine lettering 30736 Excalibur comes off the turntable at Bournemouth in 1949. We catch sight of her next in the rows awaiting shopping at Eastleigh snuggling up to 30741 Joyous Gard. *Both: Colour Rail*

As built this batch of engines were regarded as poor steamers and efforts were made during 1924 towards rectifying this with improved draughting. The board of the Southern Railway had appointed a new press and publicity officer and they decided against the wishes of Maunsell that these locomotives should be included within the King Arthur class. It has been reported that Maunsell suggested that by adding these names would not make them better performers. To further those earlier efforts towards improving some of this batch Bulleid who succeeded Maunsell decided they should try them with a multiple jet blast pipe and a larger chimney as fitted to both 30736 Excalibur opposite and to 30737 King Uther see above. Indeed, if we compare them both further we can see that the former has vertical smoke deflectors rather than the standard inwardly inclined versions. Although confined service wise to the Western Section as here with 30737 on her home shed at Bournemouth on 24 July 1951, both 30736 and 30737 would be sent to Brighton Works for scrapping when they were both withdrawn in 1956. *Chris Davies Collection/Rail Photoprints*

Being withdrawn from service during the fifties has certainly added to the rarity value in sourcing photographs for some of these 'Urie Arthurs,' although most managed as many service miles as their superior steaming and later withdrawn sisters with them all recording over 1,000,000 miles, among the highest being attributed to 30738 King Pellinore with 1,460,218 miles. Here she stands smartly turned out at Basingstoke on 29 September 1957, six months away from another rapid withdrawal and scrapping at Eastleigh in early March 1958. *Colour Rail*

Setting off from the Farnborough stop on 7 July 1950, 30739 *King Leodegrance* is on a run of the mill duty for Nine Elms' Urie Arthurs at this time with a Waterloo to Salisbury stopper. A transfer to Bournemouth would follow a few weeks before Christmas to see her out until withdrawn on 4 May 1957 and promptly cut up at Eastleigh Works within a fortnight. *E.C. Griffith/Rail Archive Stephenson*

Evidence of limescale from the Reading area's notorious hard water supplies shows around the safety valves on 30740 Merlin near Southcote Junction close to the Berkshire market town with an inter-regional service in the early fifties. She would be taken out of traffic on 10 December 1955 and sent to Brighton Works for disposal six months later. Interestingly to alleviate locomotive shortages she was sent to the LNER at Heaton between early 1943 and that September. Although Merlin seems to be scarce photographically, 30741 Joyous Gard is rarer still. The large Bulleid chimney does nothing for her looks as she lumbers gently along near Farnborough in June 1955. Her record shows her as being both withdrawn and scrapped the week ending 18 February 1956. *Photos: Anistr.com & Colour Rail*

With a hybrid version of her previously colourful Southern Railway livery still carried in July 1951, 30742 Camelot shuffles through her home town of Bournemouth's Central station. Lining up the tender lettering with cabside number throws the appearance of the tender's lines out of balance.
Anistr.com

Two views of 30743 Lyonnesse, the first dated as 30 May 1953 shows her still in lined Southern Railway malachite but without any form of tender lettering as she awaits entry to Eastleigh Works for a general overhaul which would send her back out to service in lined green. She would run in this condition at Bournemouth shed only until 6 October 1955.
Photos: *Strathwood & Colour Rail*

No doubt the yard foreman at Basingstoke will send someone out to clear away the ash piles soon, but on 12 March 1955 30744 Maid of Astolat stands by the coaling stage with her safety valves fizzing ready for her next turn today. This would be her last year in traffic still as a 70A Nine Elms locomotive just now but her last two months would see her based here at Basingstoke before being despatched to Brighton Works and broken up by early February 1956. *Strathwood Library Collection*

Previously for 745 Tintagel having been one of a number of locomotives converted briefly to oil burners in 1947, a recall to Eastleigh Works for classified repairs in late November saw her returned as a coal burner, along with the addition of her new Southern Region running number 30745 to her cab-sides along with her smokebox numberplate. The identity of the old company remained on her Malachite paintwork until her full repaint into lined Brunswick green in the summer of 1951. Here she waits for release off the coal road at Nine Elms having just been under the 'cenotaph' already on 22 June 1950.
Colour Rail

Precautions against another coal shortage have been laid aside here at Bournemouth shed wisely by the foreman alongside 30746 Pendragon when photographed sometime between her transfer to 71A Eastleigh in December 1950 and her withdrawal on 22 October 1955. Once more little time would be wasted in breaking her up at the works as she was stripped bare within a month. *Colour Rail*

Eastleigh's substantial water tower dominates 30747 Elaine simmering on shed around 1954. She was another one of ten of these Urie Arthurs to have done their bit as part of their war service for the LNER, all being based at Heaton various times during 1943. Brighton Works would become her last resting place in early May 1957, seven months after being withdrawn from here at Eastleigh shed. *Rail Photoprints*

The conduits for the electric lighting fitted to 30748 Vivien show up well in this scene at Waterloo while she awaits the off with a semi-fast for Basingstoke on 7 July 1957. In the Arthurian legend stories Vivien was the Lady of the Lake, so perhaps it was a shame that this was not added to her nameplates. It was however a name previously associated with the former LNWR and LMS. This unfortunate N15 would be taken out of service exactly two months later before a swift send-off courtesy of the cutters at Eastleigh Works by early October. Another of the class to do their final work from Basingstoke shed was 30749 Iseult. On 9 September 1956 she was photographed here at Farnborough once more soon to be sent away to Eastleigh Works for breaking nine moths later. The interesting name comes from the wife of King Mark of Cornwall who favoured one of the Knights of the Round Table within the Arthurian legend. *Photos: C.R.L. Cole/Rail Archive Stephenson & Colour Rail*

All appears well as 30750 Morgan le Fay leaves Winchfield working a Waterloo to Salisbury train on 20 April 1949. However, a glance at her record suggests she may have been a wrong 'en as she was sent from pillar to post eight times around Southern Region sheds in as many years during her short British Railways career which ended promptly again at Eastleigh Works in the summer of 1957. Opposite, 30751 Ettare appears in good fettle ready to depart Waterloo during May 1953, she would be another one slain during the summer of 1957 at Eastleigh.
Photos: E.C. Griffith/Rail Archive Stephenson & Neville Stead Collection/The Transport Library

As another of the early casualties to the scrappers, 30752 Linette is likewise a rare bird in front of the cameramen of the day. Withdrawn on 10 December 1955 and swiftly dismantled within Brighton's workshops, it was a pleasure to come across this view of her at Southampton with a stopper from Bournemouth taken in the early fifties. *The Transport Treasury*

Opposite: A return to the platforms at Waterloo during May 1953 also finds 30753 Melisande tucked away waiting to change platform roads to move onto her next working. Perhaps she was another problem child having worked her way through eight transfers during her British Railways days too, until withdrawn in March 1957.
Neville Stead Collection/The Transport Library

Destined to be by far the rarest on film during her noticeably short British Railways career would be 30754 The Green Knight as she was withdrawn on 10 February 1953 and taken apart at Eastleigh within a fortnight of this date. This shot of the rarest Arthur of them all most likely dates from around 1952 of it passing Malden at speed, this station became New Malden during 1957. *Strathwood Library Collection*

Aside from being adorned with a larger crest on her tender initially in April 1950, 30755 The Red Knight was highly regarded as the best of the bunch having been given Bulleid pattern cylinders, Lemaitre multiple blast pipe chimney and being fitted with vertical smoke deflectors rather than the standard curved inwards variety. The larger crest was replaced by a smaller one before being withdrawn on 11 May 1957. This is how she appeared on 2 June 1951 trotting away past the entrance to the works at Eastleigh where she would be scrapped exactly six years later. *Colour Rail*

The first of the next batch of the class 30763-30792 were built during 1925 by the North British Locomotive Co. in Glasgow and became known as a result as the 'Scotch Arthurs' or 'Scotsmen'. Their cabs were modified to suit the narrower loading gauge of the Eastern Section and fitted with eight-wheel bogie tenders. Going well near Weybridge around 1955, 30763 Sir Bors de Ganis is showing a feather from her safety valves, she had just transferred away from the Eastern and Central Sections for the first time in her career and would remain allocated here on the Western Section until being sent to Eastleigh for scrap in October 1960. An easier life appears onboard 30764 Sir Gawain as she passes the former Great Western Railway's Radipole Halt as they approach Weymouth with a local train from Bournemouth during September 1957.
Photos: Rail Online & T.G. Hepburn/Rail Archive Stephenson

There is nothing much to hinder the progress of 30765 Sir Gareth on this sunny winter's day on 14 December 1958 near Winchfield. Allocated now to Basingstoke shed she would be a regular through here on semi-fast duties and goods turns to Nine Elms or Feltham until her dismissal on 29 September 1962, the cutters would make short work of her in the same way as her sisters as she would gone for good by the middle of November. *Colour Rail*

A combination of electrification to the Kent Coast along with an influx of Standard 4-6-0s and spare Bulleid Pacifics and Maunsell Schools would see the King Arthurs become rarer on the Eastern Section. Permanent way workers take a well-earned breather to watch the passing of 30766 Sir Geraint at Shortlands not so long before she was withdrawn on 27 December 1958. There would be no reprieve with work on the Western Section and she would be scrapped completely here at Eastleigh soon after this photograph was taken on 24 January 1959. *Both: Colour Rail*

Opposite: Rostered for this holiday makers special for Ramsgate in August 1956, 30767 Sir Valence has her injectors on as she passes Whitstable. Originally this locomotive was to have been named as Sir Mordred. *Bluebell Museum Archive*

The rather delicious early British Railways hybrid malachite livery of 30768 Sir Balin as seen at Dover was worn until her overhaul in May/June 1952, when her standardised lined green livery would be applied. *Rail Online*

Leaving a trail of smoky exhaust across Denmark Hill station on 8 August 1953, 30769 Sir Balan from Stewarts Lane heads this Victoria to Ramsgate working. She would remain based at the lane until June 1959 when she was re-allocated to the Western Section too swiftly see out her time. Withdrawn officially on 27 February 1960, but it seems the Eastleigh cutters had already despatched her a fortnight previously. Eking out her last days on shed at Eastleigh on 9 September 1962 was the soon to be Basingstoke based 30770 Sir Prianius, although her final re-allocation would just last for four weeks before being withdrawn. Back here to Eastleigh she would be sent to join the now large numbers of redundant steam locomotives awaiting scrapping here in early 1963. **Photos: Colour Rail & Michael Morant Collection**

The superb condition of 30771 Sir Sagramore back here at her home shed of Dover suggests this photograph was taken soon after being repaired at Ashford Works and put back into traffic on 19 May 1950. *Rail Online*

Our first shot of 30772 Sir Percivale in the lines at Eastleigh in the hybrid early British Railways malachite was taken some time between April 1948 and October 1949 during the brief period she carried this scheme. Next we catch sight of her at her final home shed at Bournemouth still wearing the smaller version of the early BR emblem on 20 May 1961, less than five months from being withdrawn.

Photos: Strathwood Library Collection & Colour Rail

Opposite: Eastleigh shed staff are keeping 30773 Sir Lavaine fit on this local working at Parkstone during 1961 for something to do, hardly testing work. However, it was keeping her going to become one of the last Arthurs still at work into 1962, the glory of express work having long passed for the class, save for failures or specials. *Colour Rail*

Freshly spruced up and renumbered 30774 Sir Gaheris retains her colourful lined Malachite livery after repairs at Eastleigh during April 1949, Brunswick green would be applied during her next works visit three years later. She would get five further overhauls here to see her through until 9 January 1960 and her final visit to Eastleigh for breaking up. *Colour Rail*

Opposite: Having just passed Sandling Junction on 1 August 1957, 30775 Sir Agravaine heads for Victoria with an up-boat train. Interestingly when this example was transferred away from Dover shed on 14 June 1959, she was sent to work the remainder of her days out of 70B Feltham on goods turns. This only lasted a short while as she was declared as withdrawn and cut up the week ending 27 February the year after at Eastleigh Works.
K.L. Cook/Rail Archive Stephenson

Parked out the back of Ashford shed on 24 March 1956 was 30776 Sir Galagars, no doubt stopped for repairs, although she had her last heavy intermediate overhaul just six-months previously. There would be no transfer away from the Eastern & Central Section in British Railways days for this one, based at Dover from 5 February 1951 until withdrawn on 21 January 1959 and sent to Eastleigh Works surplus to requirements.
J.F. Davies/Rail Archive Stephenson

Opposite: The sole lucky escapee from the scrappers is seen in her early post-nationalisation hybrid malachite livery guise on a Waterloo to Bournemouth working on 15 April 1949. She would be another example sent to 70B Feltham for goods work in June 1959, but rather than be sent for scrap afterwards she found sanctuary from 5 October 1960 at Basingstoke until withdrawn and set aside as part of the National Collection after 21 October 1961. *E.C. Griffith/Rail Archive Stephenson*

There would be no such reprieve for 30778 Sir Pelleas seen alongside 30747 Elaine at Waterloo waiting to set off for Southampton Docks with a boat train from Waterloo on 17 June 1954. Dover shed had given the locomotive up in favour of 70A Nine Elms on 20 July the previous year ensuring she would be a regular around the capital until being sent for scrap at Eastleigh after 23 May 1959, her duties done with 1,174,925 miles to her credit. **Rail Online**

Setting out for Salisbury with a stopper and away from Andover Junction on 14 May 1955 is 30779 Sir Colgrevance from the 70A Nine Elms allocation. When the locomotive was new she had worn her number as E779, the E denoting Eastleigh as her parent works at a time when the Southern Railway chose to denote such matters as part of their numbering system, with A for Ashford and B for Brighton. *R.C. Riley/The Transport Library*

The earlier repaints into British Railways lined green seem to have made use of the larger style of new emblem in this fashion as worn by 30780 Sir Persant on shed at Nine Elms on 16 September 1950, having been repainted from her wartime black livery into what was reported as a lighter version of malachite livery by the Southern Railway in March 1947 which was retained until her overhaul into this condition after early January 1950.
Neville Stead Collection/The Transport Library

Opposite: Running with her British Railways number and her Southern heritage still declared upon her tender 30781 Sir Aglovale is seen near Weald around 1949.
Rail Archive Stephenson

Two views of 30782 Sir Brian taken at Eastleigh during 1962 shortly before being taken out of service on 15 September.
Both: Strathwood Library Collection

She would be the first of her class to wear the standardised British Railways lined Brunswick green livery when 30783 Sir Gillemere was outshopped on 29 July 1949, proudly displaying the new nationalised company's crest as here soon afterwards in the shed yard at Nine Elms.
Strathwood Library Collection

Opposite: A fairly moderate goods working has befallen the crew of 30784 Sir Nerovens when seen near Reading West on 2 May 1959. This locomotive had been fitted with an odd and ugly larger diameter chimney from June 1947 until May 1948, then modified again and further evaluated from early 1949 until October 1954. ***Colour Rail***

This shot of 30785 Sir Mador de la Porte in steam awaiting a call to action likely dates from 1958, she now wears the later style of emblem, but not for much longer as she was noted in the long lines of stored engines awaiting either repairs or scrap alongside the shed here the following summer. The decision was not favourable and made officially on 17 October 1959 with the scrappers completing their task within the next 30 days. *Colour Rail*

Our first view of 30786 Sir Lionel was most likely taken in early October 1948 just after she had been renumbered and now awaits a return to service once more alongside Eastleigh's works. In the second she is still in malachite green beneath the filth, but the SOUTHERN lettering appears to have been painted over by 26 July 1951, once again at Eastleigh. The full lined green livery would be applied as part of her December 1952 general overhaul.
Photos: *Strathwood Library Collection & Rail Photoprints*

Right: Another small livery and numbering variation soon after nationalisation was applied to Sir Menadeuke in becoming s787 in early March 1948. The correct number of 30787 was applied a year later retaining the malachite livery. ***Strathwood***

Left: The fully approved lined Brunswick green livery was applied in November 1950 and as seen here by the Ashford coal stage is how she would stay until withdrawn on the last day of February 1959 as another for Eastleigh to dispose of. ***Colour Rail***

On 3 September 1960, 30788 Sir Urre of the Mount simmers happily on shed at Bournemouth. The less graceful name of Sir Beumains was to have been the original choice for the locomotive. Most of its time after nationalisation would be spent on the Western Section, with 71A Eastleigh as its home shed from 5 February 1951. Upon withdrawal on 10 February 1962, she had been dumped at Ashford Works for several weeks already and would be swiftly broken up within a week of being declared as withdrawn here. *Colour Rail*

The signals in the back ground here at Eastleigh show that 30789 Sir Guy has a clear road ahead after the station on this day sometime in the mid-fifties. Also, in the background can be seen the engine sheds and the works lays to the left. This is where 30789 Sir Guy would ultimately succumb to the cutters in the final days of 1959. *Rail Online*

Eastleigh's 30790 Sir Villiars cuts a fine sight as she awaits departure from Waterloo on 6 July 1957 in her well-presented condition. She had been through a heavy intermediate overhaul less than five months beforehand and the opportunity to apply the then newer form of tender emblem was also taken. The locomotive would manage better than average mileage for the class with 1,404,162 showing on her record card upon withdrawal on 4 November 1961. *Rail Photoprints*

Opposite: Taken not so long after its last general overhaul completed during February 1957, 30791 Sir Uwaine still looks well-oiled on shed at Eastleigh. The later emblem would be affixed to the tender in November 1959 just in time it seems for the engine to be withdrawn on 21 May 1960. *Colour Rail*

Maybe one or both of today's crew of 30792 Sir Hervis de Revel were a bit nervous of her ability to swallow coal, judging by the generous load she has piled into her tender at Ramsgate on 6 April 1953, she would be the last of the Scotch Arthurs to be built. ***The Transport Treasury***

The next fourteen Arthurs were all built at Eastleigh Works during 1926, with the final two entering service in January 1927. They were destined for the Central Section and the Brighton lines who had smaller turntables in many locations, along with shorter runs in-between chances to refill both water and coal. As a result, they were designed with six-wheeled tenders, as seen on 30794 Sir Ector de Maris opposite at Brighton on 6 September 1959. The six-wheel tender for 30793 Sir Ontzlake had already been swopped over from the withdrawn 30776 Sir Galagars on 23 September 1959 to suit it better working here on the Western Section, first out of Feltham and then here at Basingstoke on 23 March 1962.
Photos: RCTS Archive & Bluebell Museum Archive

Another example also now coupled to a larger eight-wheeled tender was 30795 Sir Dinadan on 29 May 1958, just one month after her general overhaul and being attached to the ex-Urie tender from 30738 King Pellinore. This view taken at Stewarts Lane serves to show the modest difference in the engine's frame level and that of the earlier tender. Whereas 30796 Sir Dodinas le Savage is still paired to her original tender leaving Cannon Street on 30 May 1958, however she would complete her service career matched to the tender from 30766 Sir Geraint after 7 January 1961 for her last fourteen months of work based out of Salisbury. *Photos: Rail Photoprints & R.C. Riley/The Transport Treasury*

It was almost as though the Southern Railway intentionally began repainting some of their express locomotives into malachite livery during 1947 from their previous wartime black in an attempt to keep their old ways alive after the forthcoming nationalisation. One of these was 797 Sir Blamor de Ganis outshopped as such in mid-October 1947. Transition into 30797 came in late January 1949, with the old company's name painted over as seen here on 11 July 1950 at Ashford. A general overhaul in the autumn of 1951 resulted in lined Brunswick green embellished with the smaller British Railways emblem being affixed to her tender. *J.M. Jarvis/Online Transport Archive/Rail Archive Stephenson*

By 17 September 1950 when 30798 Sir Hectimere was seen at Tonbridge she was adorned with a larger crest on her tender to set off the new livery applied during November the previous year. As the crew set about their preparation task at Nine Elms the larger tender from the withdrawn 30450 Sir Kay, which had previously come from the likewise withdrawn 30737 King Uther originally was now in tow.
Photos: Bluebell Museum Archive & Barry Lewis

The story for 30799 Sir Ironside would be different as she would retain her six-wheeled tender to the end, even though a transfer on 14 June 1959 would make her a Salisbury locomotive up until withdrawn on 25 February 1961. In earlier days as a Bricklayers Arms allocated engine, she has command of an early Sunday evening Newhaven to Victoria boat train on 13 April 1958 near Lewes. *Bluebell Museum Archive*

Opposite: Whereas 30800 Sir Meleaus de Lile photographed charging through Gravesend with her safety valves blowing on 14 June 1959 would be a different story with regards to tenders. The first swap came with exchanging six-wheel tenders from 30795 Sir Dinadan in December 1953, next doing likewise with 30801 Sir Meliot de Logres in December 1958, before settling upon this eight-wheel example inherited from 30454 Queen Guinevere a few weeks later on 10 January 1959. **Colour Rail**

Looking clean and with steam to spare, 30801 Sir Meliot de Logres draws a mid-afternoon service from Ramsgate into Ashford on 3 May 1958. There would be no Western Section reprieve as she was withdrawn as a Bricklayers Arms engine after being sent to Eastleigh for assessment or repair in April 1959. The fortunes of 30802 Sir Durnore would be better as she acquired the larger tender from 30750 Morgan le Fay upon transfer to Stewarts Lane in June 1958, as a result when transferred on again to Eastleigh a year later, they thought kindlier of her and kept her in traffic for another twenty-five months. This is her raising some echoes through Folkstone Warren with a late afternoon Margate to Charing Cross service on 15 May 1952.
Photos: *Colour Rail & Bluebell Museum Archive*

Two views of 30803 Sir Harry le Fisk Lake at both ends of its British Railway's career, firstly in Malachite green at Ashford between July 1948 and November 1951. Finally paired with the tender from 30792 Sir Hervis de Revel and relegated to goods turns on shed at Feltham in September 1960.
Photos: Anistr.com & Colour Rail

A lovely detail study of 30804 Sir Cador of Cornwall at rest on her home shed at Eastleigh on 11 September 1960, strangely she went to Ashford Works for scrap in mid-February the following year. *Colour Rail*

Soon to be transferred away from Dover shed to her new home at Eastleigh in two months' time, 30805 Sir Constantine gets a work out in this up parcel train at Ashford on 13 April 1959. There would be no call to swap the tender to an eight-wheel one as once on the Western Section she would soon fall surplus to requirements in late November and be gone forever thanks to the works cutting staff before Christmas 1959. *Colour Rail*

The imminent demise of steam on Kent coast duties attracted a number of cameramen to record what they could before it passed into memory, such as here at Chatham with a well turned out 30806 Sir Galleron making a grand entrance on 17 January 1959. In 1944 this Arthur had a close shave with a German V1 doodlebug which took out a road over bridge near Newington in Kent and derailed her. The wreckage was loaded into four wagons and dragged to Eastleigh for repairs, she was back in traffic by mid-January. Based at Hither Green for most of the fifties her tender was changed to an eight-wheel one from the already withdrawn Maunsell Class N15X 32331 Beattie, during 30806's overhaul at Eastleigh during August 1958.
Colour Rail

Maunsell's Sea Dogs

Faced with dealing with heavier trains from London to the Channel ports and the West Country, Richard Maunsell sought to make progress on his already improved version of Robert Urie's King Arthur 4-6-0s. The result was 850 built at Eastleigh during 1925 and given the name Lord Nelson. For a fleeting time, it was the most powerful steam locomotive in Great Britain. Further changes were made to valves, cylinders, tenders, boilers, smoke deflectors by Maunsell at first and then by his successor, the most obvious externally by Oliver Bulleid was to the chimney with the large diameter type seen opposite at Eastleigh's coal stage on 2 June 1951. A view from behind that impressive tender at Nine Elms a couple of years beforehand in 1949, reveals the Southern Railways' sunshine style of lettering as first applied to the new nationalised railway to the south of the Thames.
Photos: *Rail Online & Colour Rail*

The larger cabside numbering gave way to this smaller less cramped style seen above and opposite, although the use of the smaller sized British Railways emblems on such a large tender was avoided thankfully. Above we see 30850 Lord Nelson setting off with a morning train for Basingstoke from Waterloo in June 1954. As with 30453 King Arthur the needless class reference on the nameplate was also avoided. When recorded with this low angle shot at Eastleigh around 1960, thankfully the decision to save her for the National Collection, had already been made by the time of her withdrawal on 18 August 1962. *Photos: J.D. Mills/Rail Archive Stephenson & Strathwood Library Collection*

LORD · NELSON

Entering service twenty-one months after the first of the class, 30851 Sir Francis Drake was a regular to be seen here at its home shed of Eastleigh as witnessed in August 1956. After failing a boiler inspection in September 1961, she was stored in the nearby works until declared withdrawn three months later. *The Transport Treasury*

Opposite: Brewing up nicely at Bournemouth in preparation for its next run to London or back home most likely to Eastleigh on 21 April 1956 we find 30852 Sir Walter Raleigh. Just two of the Nelsons would be scrapped at Ashford Works, with 30863 Lord Rodney being the other. *R.C.T.S. Archive*

Originally this first batch of ten locomotives were substituted for King Arthur production, some of which were to go to the Eastern Section, as a result of this and subsequent works visits tender swaps became commonplace before World War Two. Tucked in amongst the usual que of engines by the offices beneath that huge water tank at Eastleigh in her last year or so of service was 30853 Sir Richard Grenville around 1961. *Rail Online*

Opposite: No high visibility vests back in 1957 to help to protect this duo as 30854 Howard of Effingham goes sailing past a speed on the down fast line at Raynes Park on 8 August. The locomotive looks unaffected by falling down the embankment near Shawford in July 1952, which entailed some elaborate recovery work to recover it for repairs at nearby Eastleigh Works. Thankfully, the locomotive crew scrambled clear from the wreckage and lived to tell the tale no doubt many times in the loco men's mess afterwards. *Tony Butcher*

An ex-works view of 30855 Robert Blake alongside the coaling facilities at Eastleigh on 12 August 1955, straight after her general overhaul. If only they looked like this all the time? This works visit saw her sent back out with the now preferred smaller cabside numerals being applied, less convenient perhaps for visually challenged spotters with glasses passing engine sheds at speed on fast moving trains and trying to record engine numbers.
J. Robertson/The Transport Treasury

An early livery interpretation for 30856 Lord St. Vincent at Bournemouth West in the spring of 1948 with 6" numbers and 9" lettering looks odd, no smokebox number instead it was painted on the buffer beam at the front and on the back of the tender in the rear. So much smarter outside Eastleigh Works on 18 September 1960. *Both: Colour Rail*

Newly turned out in lined Brunswick green 30857 Lord Howe passes Farnborough with a lunchtime express from Waterloo on 7 July 1950. The lining on the tender can just be made out to follow the whole flared shape of the tender, similarly, seen on 30856, 30861 and 30865 at various times during this decade. Strangely the larger tender emblem was changed on this example to a smaller version between July 1952 and August 1955.
E.C. Griffith/Rail Archive Stephenson

Opposite: Originally just before the Second World War Flaman speed recorders were fitted to the entire class, however they were removed within a few years, it was not until December 1959 that speedometers were once again being fitted to the Nelsons, but not them all 30854, 30859 and 30863-5 along with 30858 Lord Duncan seen observing the speed restriction through Clapham Junction in March 1959 would all miss out.
Photos: Strathwood Library Collection & Colour Rail

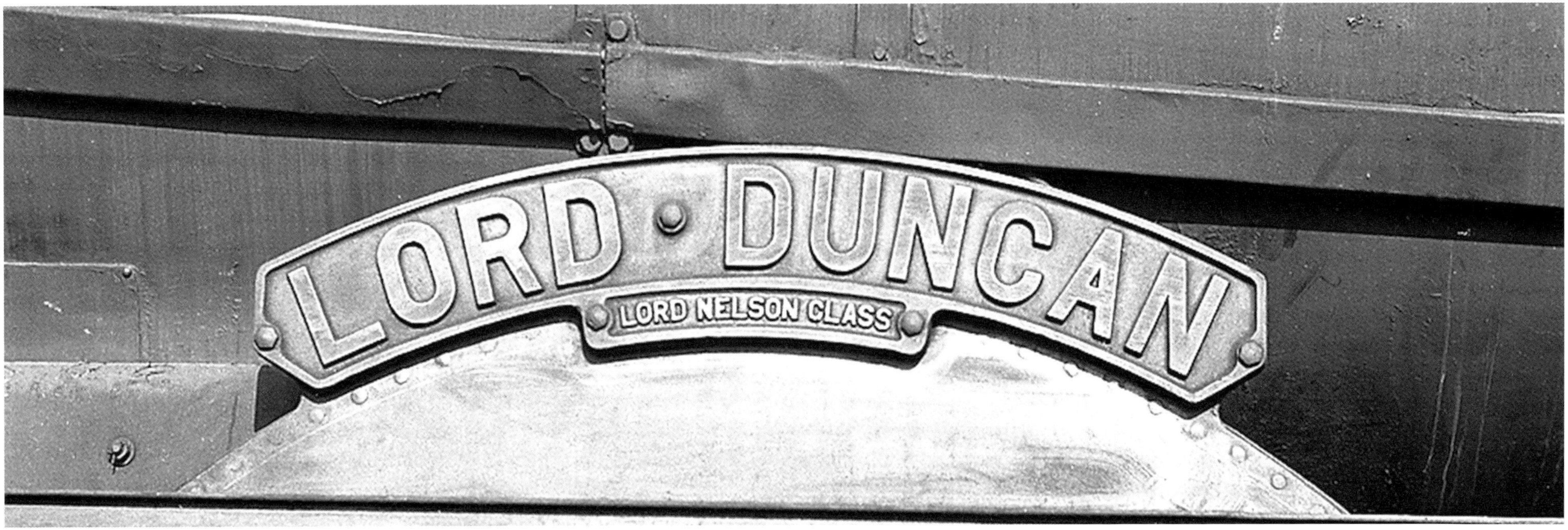
LORD DUNCAN
LORD NELSON CLASS

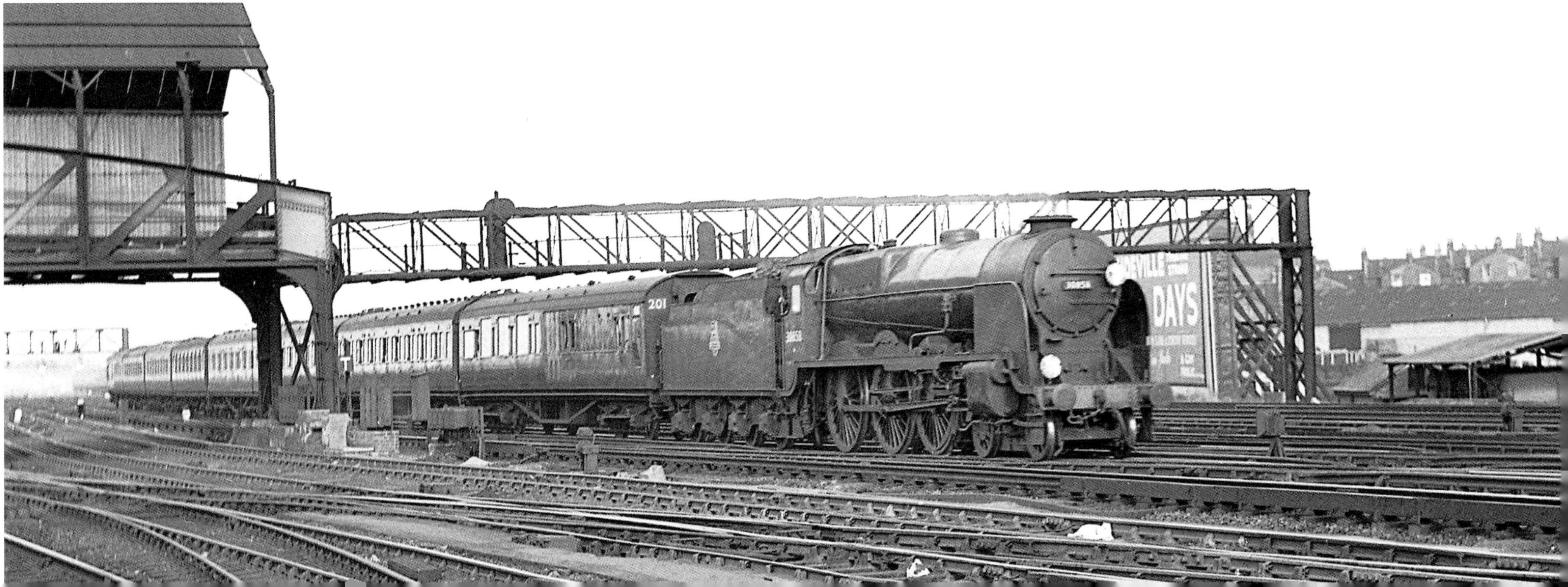
201
DAYS

The familiar setting of Worting Junction with some fellow enthusiasts greets the driver of 30859 Lord Hood as he takes the Winchester route around 1961 heading for Bournemouth. The class were also to be seen working from Bournemouth, via Reading, and Didcot as far as Oxford on inter-regional workings, sharing duties with Arthurs and Bulleid Pacifics. The AWS battery box seen on the running plate was only fitted in September 1959, indeed the whole class save for 30865 Sir John Hawkins would all be so fitted by May 1961. The exception was withdrawn the same month so missed out on another important safety feature. *Colour Rail*

Keeping Western Region company at Weymouth on 27 April 1950 was 30860 Lord Hawke, a resident of Nine Elms at this time. A transfer to Bournemouth came in June 1958, before ending her days based here at Eastleigh from 26 November 1959 until withdrawn on 11 August 1962 and cut up almost immediately.
Both: Strathwood Library Collection

Not usual territory for a Nelson, but on a cold and inclement 2 September 1962 we find 30861 Lord Anson here at Exeter Central as part of the Southern Counties Touring Society's South Western Limited. Substituting for the recently withdrawn 30850 Lord Nelson, this became the last rail tour to use both a Nelson and indeed an Arthur, as 30770 Sir Prianius also shared some of the tour. A last gasp really for the Nelson as the last two 30861 and 30862 were both withdrawn a few weeks later on 6 October. *Tony Butcher*

Opposite: How the once mighty have fallen, as 30862 Lord Collingwood runs tender first on a fill in duty with a local trip goods approaching Bournemouth Central on 11 June 1953, possibly just a running in turn after some local repairs. The view shows not only the space for the fireirons, but also the auxiliary vacuum reservoirs. The over-fill of coal behind the bunker might come in useful after all as the tender looks otherwise low on coal, but just how far would this duty take Lord Collingwood anyway? **Anistr.com**

Lord Collingwood led a line of ships under Lord Nelson in 1805 at Trafalgar, taking full command after Nelson's death.
Colour Rail

Our award for the rarest photographically of the Lord Nelsons goes to 30863 Lord Rodney, seen here running light engine at Surbiton on 9 April 1956. This view also serves to show the piano style cover to the front of the Maunsell cylinders beneath the smokebox door, the only one to retain them. Somehow strange as she sustained serious enough front-end collision damage in 1956 to see her left-hand cylinder renewed and repairs that required the front end to be renewed. Earlier in August 1949, 30863 Lord Rodney became the first of the class to be repainted into the standardised lined Brunswick green livery, retaining a red background to her nameplates. Variously the background to nameplates appeared as either red or black at differing times, modellers beware! *Tony Butcher*

Opposite: Among these livery variations we should not forget the three locomotives repainted into an apple green livery with a contrasting red, yellow and grey lining applied. The three thus painted were 30856, 30861 and 30864 Sir Martin Frobisher during the early summer of 1948. The last example is seen here drawing a crowd within Southampton Docks that July with a Pullman car Royal Boat Train special. ***Colour Rail***

A comparison of front ends can be made between 30753 Melisande stabled in the carriage sidings at Bournemouth West as 30864 Sir Martin Frobisher sets off for Waterloo on 3 September 1955. ***Colour Rail***

Ready to enter Eastleigh Works in late March 1961 for what would be the final time, we find the last built member of the class 30865 Sir John Hawkins, showing signs of some recent hard running on her smokebox. Things must have been not so great once inspected by the works staff as she was withdrawn on 30 May. A start was made on cutting her up the following month, but she was still reported as identifiable in the cutting area it seems into August. With this first example now withdrawn and promptly scrapped, fifteen of the sixteen strong class would swiftly follow as the Southern Region divested itself of steam, with five more being withdrawn during 1961, three of them also being broken up that same year including 30854, 30858 and 30859.
Colour Rail

We take a final look at 30865 Sir John Hawkins a few weeks previously that final winter, hard at work passing Eastleigh's running shed with a rake of coal empties. By the end of November 1962, just 30850 Lord Nelson remained in tact set aside for preservation. Restoration would be a long time in coming as 30850 was split from her tender and stored firstly in the old roundhouse at Fratton, then Stratford, Brighton's Pullman Works and finally to Carnforth in 1977, with restoration to working order beginning thankfully in 1979. *Colour Rail*

Lest We Forget

When the Southern Railway electrified the Brighton and Eastbourne lines in 1933 it made the six L Class 4-6-4Ts designed by Billington redundant. Frustrated with the availability of both investment and supplies of enough 4-6-0s, Maunsell set about rebuilding the tank locomotives. The tenders were taken from Urie S15s who in turn inherited tenders from withdrawn Drummond 4-4-0s. Thus, the N15X Class was created, retaining the former LBSCR class name Remembrance after 333 being named as such to honour memory of the Brighton company's men who lost their lives in the First World War. The rebuilding work was conducted at Eastleigh Works, with 329 Stephenson renumbered as 2329 being the first released in December 1934. This is 32337 Trevithick with an early afternoon Waterloo to Basingstoke near Pirbright Junction on 15 February 1955. In its days as a Baltic tank, it had been originally named Charles C Macrae. Its end would come dramatically in a collision with an electric train near Woking in the darkness of 23 December 1955 while working the 7.54pm Waterloo to Basingstoke. The twisted wreck was towed to Eastleigh Works for scrapping which was completed in 1956.
Peter Pescod/The Transport Treasury

The original Baltic tank 4-6-4Ts being built at Brighton saw them being renumbered by the Southern Railway with a 2 added to their original running numbers. A decision was made to name five of the Class N15X 4-6-0s after five of the early locomotive engineers. Given the name Hackworth we see 32328 on shed at Nine Elms around 1949/1950 retaining her Southern Railway style of Malachite livery, albeit hybridised by British Railways. The distinction of being the first of these rebuilds to be withdrawn fell upon 32328 Hackworth in February 1955. **Dave Cobbe Collection/Rail Photoprints**

Most of the work for the class kept them on the Western Section during their albeit short British Railways careers, with the entire class allocated to Basingstoke for secondary duties. Taken the same month as the second withdrawal of the class for 32330 Cudworth had just been announced, our cameraman thankfully seized upon this chance to record 32329 Stephenson alongside the lodgings block and water tank at Eastleigh in August 1955, twelve months later and 32329 likewise would follow suit. Opposite we see 32330 Cudworth still in Malachite near Woking with an up stopper from Basingstoke, she may be blowing off, but her smokebox tells another tale. **Photos: The Transport Treasury & Colour Rail**

We take a second look at 32330 Cudworth at Basingstoke on 20 March 1954 now sporting lined black livery as a mixed-traffic locomotive classified as 4P, rather than what may have looked more glamorous and attractive in a lined Brunswick green scheme. *R.C.T.S. Archive*

Opposite: This is 2331 Beattie running fast through Surbiton on 27 February 1949 retaining her Southern Railway identity and livery, the renumbering as 32331 followed that May. With one of the fixings for her smokebox numberplate having to be made through the top strap. *Colour Rail*

Now finished in lined black 32331 Beattie stands over the inspection pits at Nine Elms around 1956, by which time she was to become the last survivor, remaining in traffic until July 1957. All of the locomotive engineer names bore reference to their class with respect.
Both: Strathwood Library Collection

The bolder BR lining shows off the curves but wisely is not carried onto the smoke deflectors in the way of the original SR style, both views were taken on shed at Nine Elms in 1948 and 1954.
Rail Archive Stephenson & Strathwood

The nameplate and commemorative plaque say it all and are proudly displayed today in the National Railway Museum. The locomotive herself 32333 is seen being prepared at Nine Elms also retaining her lined malachite albeit sadly somewhat dirty with both views most likely taken in June 1951.
Photos: Colour Rail & Rail Online

Now respectfully dressed in lined black livery 32333 *Remembrance* is seen at Eastleigh awaiting works attention and what is thought to be at Basingstoke around 1952. *Both: Strathwood Library Collection*

During the Second World War, 2327-2329, 2331 & 2332 were loaned from the Southern Railway to the neighbouring Great Western Railway to assist with locomotive shortages, they returned home during 1943 having been replaced by newly delivered Stanier 8Fs and S160 2-8-0s. They returned home to the Southern based at Nine Elms, however the influx of the more powerful Bulleid Pacifics would push them aside, so that by nationalisation they were all based at Basingstoke who set them to work on Waterloo to Basingstoke semi-fast services, the class also found employment west to Salisbury and on cross-country duties taking them to Portsmouth, Brighton, Bournemouth, Reading and Oxford. When 32333 Remembrance was withdrawn in July 1956, as a matter of respect she was consigned to Brighton Works who removed her nameplates and plaques for display within the works, before she was broken up. Another missed opportunity of course, but it must be recognised the British Transport Commission only set up a committee to select significant locomotives to form the National Collection in 1960. **Colour Rail**

Paddleboxes

There were ten of these Class T14 4-6-0s designed and built during Dugald Drummond's reign as CME of the LSWR. In their original guise with heavy side splashers complete with a porthole access, they acquired the nickname of 'Paddleboxes' although in some quarters they were also known as 'Double Breasters.' This first undated photograph at Nine Elms of 447 alongside 34023 Blackmore Vale (1948 spelling) was taken around the summer of 1949. Perversely 447 was renumbered as 30447 in November 1949 and promptly withdrawn the following month. Whereas 30446 being attended to at Feltham in October 1949, had been renumbered during August the previous year and would soldier on until May 1951.
Photos: Rail Photoprints & TOPticl.com

Drummond's 4-6-0 classes were regarded as poor steamers unless the men knew how to handle them and their peculiar ways. During Robert Urie's tenure as CME he improved the class by fitting superheaters, followed by Richard Maunsell who rebuilt all ten with a raised running plate and much smaller splashers during 1930-1931. However, by the outbreak of war in 1939 they had all been placed in store, but the onset of hostilities gave them a new lease of life completely except for 458 which was mortally damaged during an enemy air raid one night in October 1940. One of the nine survivors to be taken into British Railways ownership in 1948 was 444, seen here at Waterloo on 20 July 1949, rostered to work the 12.54pm departure for Salisbury. *Peter Pescod/The Transport Treasury*

Withdrawn the previous month 444 stands forlorn at Eastleigh Works on 4 March 1950, she would be scrapped here the same month. Just three of the nine T14s would be renumbered, this included 30461 which although it missed out on a smokebox plate it did manage sunshine style numbers and lettering to its plain black livery here at Eastleigh on 19 August 1950. *Both: Strathwood Library Collection*

The painted number on the buffer beam can just be made out under the grime on 30461 as she does her best out of Waterloo on the approach to Vauxhall on 16 September 1950. This example would be the last to survive being withdrawn and scrapped in June the following year, with a final mileage of 1,054,620. *Colour Rail*

Opposite: Drummond also built five Class F13 4-6-0s numbers 330-334 as four-cylinder locomotives in 1905 that were doomed to failure. During 1924-1925 Maunsell had them rebuilt as two-cylinder engines to become Class H15. One of these heaves her load past Farnborough on 28 July 1951. *Colour Rail*

Chonkers

The nickname 'Chonkers' really only applied to the engines with the larger diameter boilers, although many used it right across the H15s. The power classification from 4MT changed to 4P5F in 1953. The former is seen below the number on 30333 opposite at Woking in 1951, and above when seen at Feltham on 30 August 1958, just weeks from withdrawal. Likewise, 30331 caries 4P5F above her number at Nine Elms in September 1957.
Photos: Strathwood, Colour Rail & The Transport Treasury

In their original guise as Class F13 these five engines were originally built at Nine Elms in 1905 without smoke deflectors and with smaller diameter chimneys. When 30331 was recorded here at Chichester on 20 September 1952 she was still looking well kempt sixteen months after her last overhaul. British Railways inherited them all in unlined black after the war years, prior to this they would have enjoyed the Southern's lined olive-green livery. Those days were gone when 30333 was recorded on shed at Nine Elms in her hybrid livery complete with narrower chimney. Lined black livery would follow a few months later and in 1952 a short, flared chimney would be substituted. These five would spend most of the time in BR days on the Western Section based out of Salisbury, Feltham and Nine Elms straying occasionally as we see opposite towards the Central Section. The first withdrawn would be 30332 in November 1956 and the last to work would be 30331 until March 1961, all five would perish at Eastleigh Works.

Photos: Rail Photoprints & Michael Morant Collection

There would be a further rebuild undertaken by Robert Urie from Dugald Drummond's Class E14 4-6-0 which was affected on the Nine Elms 1907 built engine in 1914, to become an additional Class H15 at Eastleigh Works, which would later become 335. Richard Maunsell improved matters once again in 1927, with a superheater being fitted to her original boiler. She was based at Salisbury in 1948 upon nationalisation and in Eastleigh Works for overhaul at the time, her release would be in a plain black livery and at first became s335 with BRITISH RAILWAYS lettering in full on her tender.

This soon changed into a lined black livery retaining the original tender lettering but now correctly numbered as 30335, complete with her smokebox numberplate. In early 1952 the first version of the new emblem was applied to her tender which would see her into retirement on 6 June 1959, this was the same month as our first photograph was taken of her dumped at Eastleigh having just been emptied of her coal. Our second picture shows her now partly dismembered by 29 August, with 1,327,650 miles of service under her belt. *Photos: Jim Oatway & Colour Rail*

Our next batch 30482-30491 were built to Urie's specifications in 1914 at Eastleigh in turn they were all rebuilt by Maunsell from 1927. Two views of the same engine here as s482 at Eastleigh on 10 June 1948 and back for the final time for scrap in June 1959.
Both: *Strathwood Library Collection*

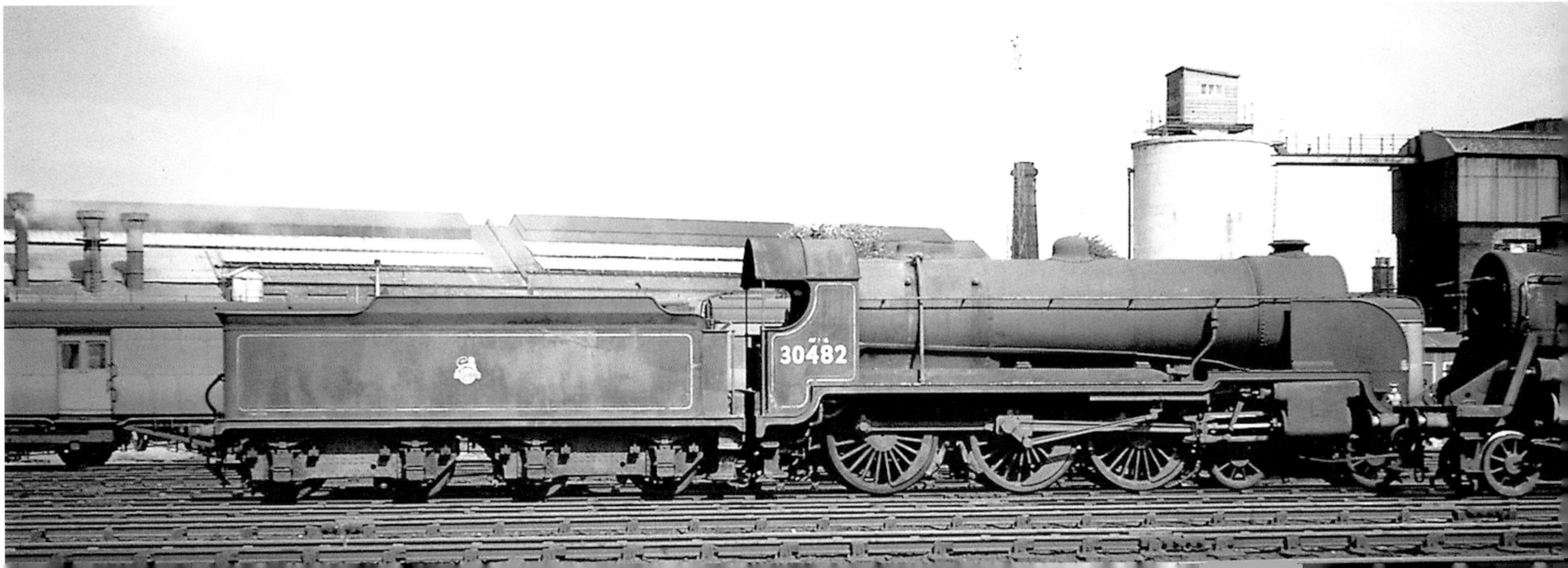

Having emerged from overhaul without either tender lettering or emblems from Eastleigh Works on 15 July 1949, 30487 caught our cameraman's attention nearby at the shed still like this a few years later on 20 September 1951. She would be recalled to works once more for a general overhaul two weeks later on 5 October to be sent back to traffic with an exchanged boiler and a repaint on 3 November, now with a smaller sized emblem in place. This is how we see her shuffling around with empty stock at Clapham Junction on 20 April the following year.
Photos: Neville Stead Collection/The Transport Library & R.C.T.S. Archive

An opportunity to play spot the differences with chimneys, domes, smoke deflectors, boilers and safety valve covers with 30482 at Nine Elms in 1958 against 30491 ex-works at Eastleigh on 11 May 1957. The latter example had been modified in 1927 to this condition, thus releasing its original boiler as a spare for numbers 482 to 490. **Both: Strathwood Library Collection**

Nine Elms allocated 30484 looks clean and tidy in the shed yard at Reading's southern establishment on 29 September 1957. She was still fresh from her last heavy intermediate overhaul and would continue to give good service until 9 May 1959. Her mileage would be an impressive 1,517,013 when scrapped at Eastleigh Works in early July the same year. *Strathwood Library Collection*

More comparisons between 30482 and 30491, firstly at Surbiton on 22 March 1957 with a service for Southampton Terminus as part of its 1,471,917-mile career. Secondly with 30491 at Dorchester West on 7 June 1958, who managed 1,539,740 miles with seventeen more months in service.
Photos: Tony Butcher & Colour Rail

The difference in the running plate between 30491 seen taking coal at Eastleigh on 17 March 1960 and her Maunsell designed sisters 30473-30478 and 30521-30524 also with N15 style boilers built three years earlier in 1924 can be seen with 521 yet to be renumbered as 30521 when recorded at Bournemouth West in 1948. *Photos: Neville Stead Collection & Strathwood Library Collection*

Two styles of hybrid H15 liveries are seen, firstly with 30522 below at Eastleigh on 11 June 1949 wearing plain black and sunshine numbers to match her tender. Also seen the same month was 30475 also in plain black however with the unimaginative Gill Sans early lettering and numbers at Exmouth Junction.
Both: Strathwood Library Collection

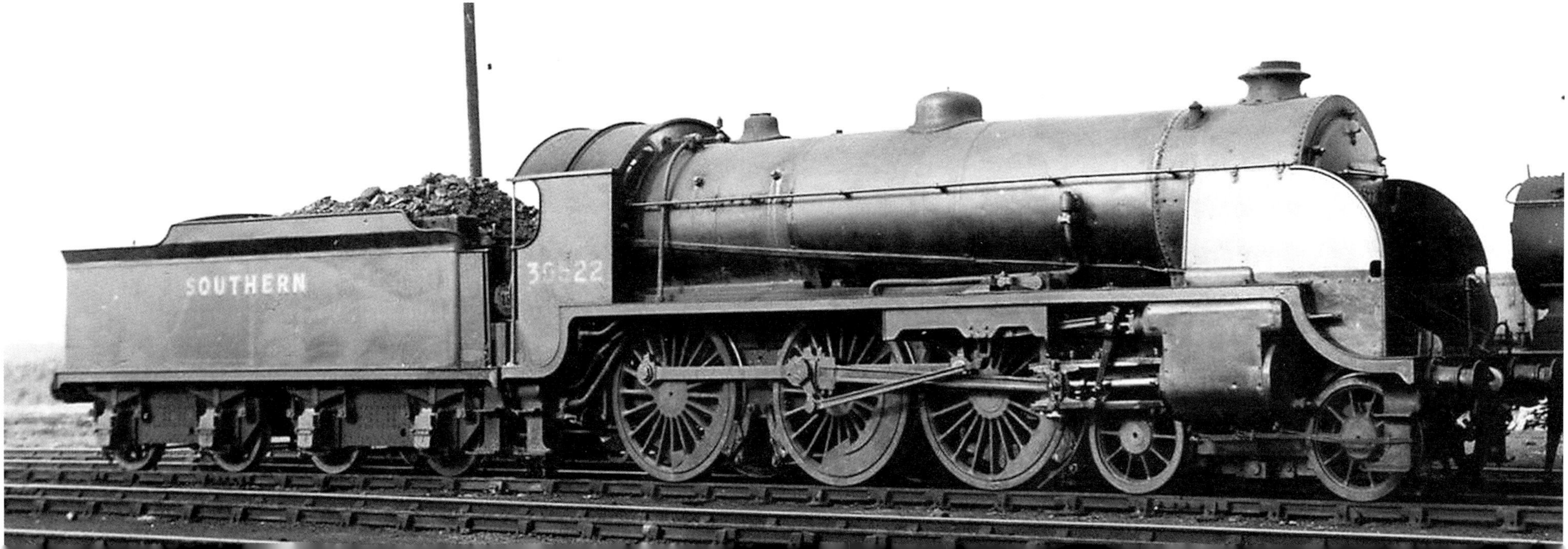

Reminders of the old company could still be seen as late as 24 July 1951 with 30474 on Bournemouth's turntable, although she would succumb to the new ways two months later. *Strathwood Library Collection*

In turn the larger versions of the early emblems would give way to the smaller ones, this is 30473 at Eastleigh on 4 September 1954 with a 5,000-gallon tender. Later on, after being paired with a slightly larger 5,200-gallon tender in August 1957 the smaller earlier emblem was affixed higher to be in line with the cabside numbers.
Strathwood Library Collection

Eastleigh allocated 30477 enjoys some passenger work at Fratton in June 1955, the ten fewer years of their service lives reflected in the final mileages too for the Maunsell H15s, with this example managing 1,020,549 when withdrawn on 4 July 1959. As it was at the time Eastleigh Works made short work of cutting her up a month later. *Peter Hay/The Transport Treasury*

A mid-fifties view of 30476 being prepared for service at Eastleigh, twenty-six H15s in all varieties were inherited by British Railways in 1948. The first two were withdrawn in 1955, with 30485 and 30490 being the first to fall. As the sixties dawned their number had dwindled to just ten examples with the final three including 30475, 30476 and 30521 bowing out in December 1961. *Rail Online*

Opposite: Southampton Terminus still looks prosperous when visited on 26 June 1957 with light engine movements for the thirty-two-year-old Class H15 30473 and the eleven-month-old newcomer in the shape of Standard 4MT 76064. *R.C. Riley/The Transport Treasury*

Another view of 30476 again on shed at Eastleigh, this time taken after her general overhaul in the works which ended on 18 January 1958 with her wearing the final style of British Railways emblems, facing forward on both sides of the tender. *Colour Rail*

Another of the final survivors 30521 gets some more mileage in on passenger work as part of her mixed-traffic status as she has her safety valves feathering nicely passing Brookwood in 1959. Trying to hold back time against the inevitable the desolate hulk of 30524 managed to stall her fate with the scrappers after being withdrawn on 25 February 1961, when she was photographed out to grass in Eastleigh's cutting area on 25 June, all would be gone however within another week. *Photos: Michael Morant Collection & Rail Online*

Urie's S15s

Having created the N15s for express passenger work, the H15s for mixed traffic use, Robert Urie then focused on a new 4-6-0 goods engine and arrived at the need for twenty Class S15 locomotives. They would all be built in the LSWR's workshops at Eastleigh during 1920-1921. When 30499 was photographed in the sunshine one day in 1959 at Salisbury she differed from her original condition, her chimney and smoke deflectors being the most obvious changes externally during Maunsell's period in charge on the Southern Railway. In the summer of 1962, she would be fitted with AWS and just a matter of weeks from being withdrawn as 1963 became 1964, she would be paired with the six-wheel 4,000-gallon tender from 30835 at Feltham.
Rail Photoprints

As the Southern Railway became the Southern Region of British Railways changes were made as required by the painters, 30504 had her new numbering in place at least on 9 July 1949 at Eastleigh. Whereas 30509 also enjoyed new lettering on her Drummond 4,000-gallon water cart tender back on shed at Feltham in June 1949. The tender from the withdrawn Class H15 30487 would replace the one on 30504 in early 1958, while 30509 would inherit the tender from N15X 32328 Hackworth when it was withdrawn early in 1955.
Both: Strathwood Library Collection

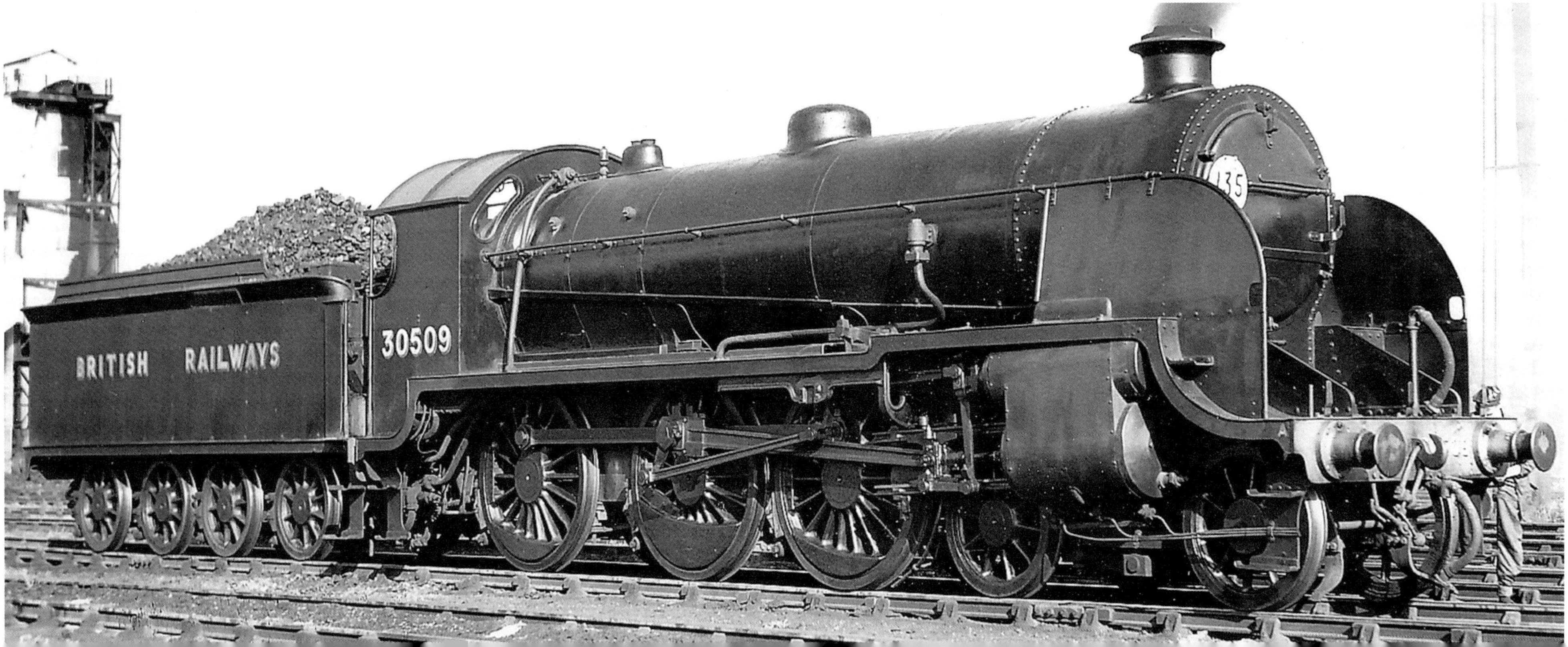

The first overhaul of 30499 post nationalisation came during December 1948, which meant that when she returned to traffic in early January a decision on the numbering style in Gill Sans had been made, along with smokebox plates being cast as required. However, rather than paint her tender with BRITISH RAILWAYS instead she left Eastleigh Works with it blank. Here she is on shed here sometime before the smaller version of the new emblem was applied after release from her next overhaul in May 1951. Others to carry blank tenders at this time included 30506, 30508, 30510 and 30512.
Strathwood Library Collection

Although the S15s had been in green livery during Southern Railway days, they all came into British Railways possession in plain black livery with the former company's lettering and numbering that was applied as they came up for repairs during the war years and post-war too. When 30513 was returned to service from an overhaul in November 1949 she acquired one of the larger early emblems with versions printed so that the lion would face forward on both sides as here at Eastleigh on 26 July 1951. *Chris Davies Collection/Rail Photoprints*

A mid-fifties scene at Eastleigh with 30506 still coupled to her Drummond water-cart tender, this would be given up in favour of the spare 5,000-gallon tender created when 30745 Tintagel was withdrawn during 1956, repainting it into unlined black and an early small emblem for a return to duty at 70B Feltham. *Strathwood Library Collection*

Previously 30505 had carried Southern style numerals, Gill Sans BRITISH RAILWAYS tender lettering and a smokebox numberplate. Fresh from a visit to the works here at Eastleigh 30505 was wearing the now approved paint scheme on 4 February 1950. Interestingly she carries a 70A shed plate which had just become Nine Elms. The Southern's three letter shed codes had just given way to this latest version influenced by the LMS. However, 30505 would need to have that plate changed as she went back into service based out of 70B Feltham, previously coded as FEL. *Strathwood Library Collection*

Two more examples from the mid-fifties with 30511 visiting Eastleigh on 12 August 1955 and 30507 at her West London home at Feltham on 11 July 1955.
Both: Strathwood

A sunny and warm day around Easter in 1958 sees 30503 ready to set off from Waterloo with what looks to be a well loaded passenger working, something the class would be often allocated towards helping out on busy holidays and summer Saturdays, maybe they should have worn lined black as their cousins the H15s did too? Around the same time Feltham allocated 30498 is also likely to work her passage back to the capital with a passenger extra after this visit to Bournemouth shed. *Photos: Tony Butcher & Colour Rail*

Goods work was their calling primarily of course, towards their last couple of years a start was made towards fitting them with AWS during 1961-1962, not all would be fitted though. These two show their battery boxes placed in front of the cab on the driver's side, with 30509 at Basingstoke and 30514 on shed at Nine Elms both taken in 1962. Whereas 30506 was still to be fitted out as such set aside alongside the shed at Feltham on 6 October the same year. She would be released from Eastleigh six weeks later fully equipped with AWS to see her through to being withdrawn week ending 5 January 1964. Feltham was no stranger to dumped withdrawn locomotives as they awaited passage to either Eastleigh or to scrap dealers. Thankfully Woodhams in Barry were the purchasers of several lots, including 30499 and 30506 who would be preserved, they also acquired 30512 but set to cutting her up soon after her arrival at Barry in January 1965. Cohen's of Kettering took four 30497, 30507, 30509 and 30514 for scrapping leaving the remaining twelve to head back to Eastleigh for disposal. ***Photos: Strathwood Library Collection & Peter Simmonds***

Looking more like it was curtains for 30500 here at Eastleigh with her rods off on 2 December 1962, especially as the first three withdrawals were just taking place with 30502, 30504 and 30505. Instead, 30500 had arrived for a light casual overhaul and would return to traffic until withdrawal called for real on 6 July 1963. Although there was a great cull of Southern Region steam locomotives towards the end of 1962, the harsh weather and its effect on the new diesels starting to arrive, led to scenes such as here at Pirbright during January 1963 ensuring 30515 would be kept on the books for now at least. **Photos: Peter Simmonds & Strathwood Library Collection**

Some of the Urie S15s working from Feltham might find themselves underneath the Eastern Region's overhead, but the arrival of the London Midland's would be a few years off when 30508 was noted at Eastleigh sporting warning flashes on her smoke deflectors at least on 2 March 1963, she had also been fitted with AWS as had 30515 opposite with warning flashes on her boiler too at Feltham also during March 1963. Whereas the next in line that day 30513 missed out completely and was withdrawn a few weeks later and sent to Eastleigh for scrapping, she still carries the cowl around her safety valves though. *Photos: Colour Rail & Strathwood Library Collection*

Opposite: With already reduced numbers and withdrawal imminent for the remaining Urie S15s, 30512 was given the honour of the first leg of the L.C.G.B. Hayling Island Farewell tour from here at Waterloo on 3 November 1963. **Colour Rail**

Left & above: The demise from traffic for 30512 came on 29 March four months later, when she was set aside in the yard at Eastleigh, which is where we see her before making what was to be unfortunately a one-way trip Woodhams at Barry, later in the year. Likewise, 30507 would be sent away for scrapping after storage here at Feltham having been withdrawn ten days before Christmas of 1963, only this time it was to George Cohen of Kettering had tendered for her and who would her.

Photos: Strathwood Library Collection

Maunsell's S15s

Richard Maunsell developed Urie's original 4-6-0 S15 design with an increased boiler pressure, reduced diameter cylinders with smaller grates, straight footplating and modified cabs. They would be built in two batches, the first fifteen in 1927-1928 followed by ten more nine years later. From the 1936 build we find s838 which would soon become 30838 going well at Winchfield on 20 April 1949. She had been in Eastleigh Works alongside 837 early in 1948 and they would both be sent out in this livery variant on the last day of February. *E.C. Griffith/Rail Archive Stephenson*

Very quickly after running as s837, she became renumbered correctly as 30837 in the same Southern Railway style of things in late April, here she is at Feltham complete with her new smokebox numberplate too, soon afterwards. From the first batch fitted with the earlier eight-wheel Maunsell tender, 30825 carried this livery version from May 1948 until March 1952, here she is at Exeter Central.
Both: Strathwood Library Collection

Gill Sans numbers and lettering were applied to 30841 in early October 1948 as they struggled to agree on liveries, being Exmouth Junction allocated meant she was on home territory when seen at Exeter Central on 15 June 1950. Although Eastleigh Works was the norm for repairs this example saw a light casual repair at Brighton Works during 1954. The smaller version of the early emblem having already been affixed during a previous overhaul at Eastleigh earlier the same year. *Bluebell Museum Archive*

Another carrying the same 1948 livery variant was 30847 seen at Axminster the same day in 1950 working an afternoon Templecombe service. One or two locomotives ran with plain black tenders including 30826, 30827, 30829, 30834, 30836, 30838, 30840, 30843 and possibly 30842 too, all before the larger emblem appeared as on 30828 at Eastleigh on 1 October 1950, having been so adorned in late 1949.
Photos: Bluebell Museum Archive & Strathwood Library Collection

The tender designs fitted to the Maunsell S15s varied during the final build from 838 to 847 were coupled with this design seen on 30839 at Eastleigh with the large emblem it carried from late 1949 until early 1954. It was a straight sided welded 5,000-gallon eight-wheel tender. These were also attached to numbers 833 to 837 before they were re-allocated onto the Central Section at various times. Having previously been released in late 1948 with a blank black painted tender, this had been designed by Urie as an eight-wheel 5,000-gallon version which had come from Class N15 766 Sir Geraint in 1929. This view dated as 2 June 1951 shows her fresh from the workshops that day at Eastleigh, but still to gain her smokebox number plate which was most likely fitted when she returned to the works eleven days later for a week to sort out minor adjustments.
Photos: Rail Online & Colour Rail

The use of the small emblems on such a large tender made them seem insignificant as worn by 30840 at Eastleigh in the earlier part of the fifties, compared with 30842 which did manage to gain the more in keeping larger emblem in October 1949 which it kept until the autumn of 1955. Here we see her likewise in the early fifties at Templecombe Upper. Many of this final 1936 built batch managed over 800,000 miles in service, the lowest was 30840 with 781,397 miles and the highest was the last to enter service 30847 with 931,829 miles.
Photos: Rail Photoprints & Strathwood Library Collection

Part of 30847's mileage feet was made with stopping trains from Salisbury to Exeter Central during the locomotive's eight-year tenancy at Salisbury between 1951 and 1959. One example of which is seen here at Honiton on 3 August 1955. After her overhaul in the early summer of 1961 30847 ran with AWS and looked a bit off after being paired with the narrower and slightly higher pitched 3,500-gallon tender from the withdrawn 30805 Sir Constantine which was painted plain black with a later emblem to match 30847, which it did not as it was narrower than the cab. Nonetheless she ran like this until withdrawn and sold to Woodhams in Barry. Rescued for preservation in 1978 she was paired with the tender from 30828 seen opposite. The Maunsell Locomotive Society approved the rebuilding of this Urie style 5,000-gallon tender to match the original flat sided version. Back to 30828 who is seen drifting through Seaton Junction during July 1956, the station yard looks prosperous with milk traffic from the adjacent dairy.
Photos: *The Transport Treasury & Rail Photoprints*

Another example of Class S15 locomotives being pressed into faster moving passenger work at Weybridge with a down Saturday extra behind 30839 from 70B Feltham, two spotters keep their notebooks up to date as the locomotive officially limited to 70mph races past. Most of the Maunsell S15s would end their days in the hands of the many hungry scrap merchants rather than Eastleigh Works which had previously been commonplace. Opposite we see 30842 around 1963 at Yeovil's Southern shed, she would be among the sixteen to head west to the host of South Wales dealers, but unfortunately not to Woodhams which otherwise may have afforded her survival into preservation today. **Photos: *Rail Online & Colour Rail***

Opposite: Numbers 30833 to 30837 found themselves paired with smaller six-wheel tenders to make things easier for them on the shorter Central Section's turntables. This example 30833 took this to extremes being paired with six different tenders during its working life. When photographed heading for Salisbury past Worting Junction in August 1962, 30833 had recently gained its final tender which was a 4,000-gallon type given up by the Schools Class 30908 Westminster in May 1962. **Rail Photoprints**

The extra length of these twenty-seven-foot long Urie and Maunsell 5,000 gallon eight-wheel tenders shows up well with 30830 from Salisbury making a stop at Yeovil Junction on 7 September 1961 as her driver shields his eyes from the sunshine looking out for his guard's starting signal.
**James Harrold/
The Transport Library**

Now coupled to the redundant tender from Schools Class, 30912 Downside in June 1962, 30837 looks smart when seen soon afterwards at Eastleigh. Comparing tender styles between 30838 seen on shed at Feltham on 12 July 1959 and the original six-wheel tender fitted to 30833, also seen at Feltham on 18 March 1962, just before she also gained her ex-Schools tender from 30908 Westminster.
Photos: Strathwood Library Collection & Rail Photoprints

Still hard at work during the harsh winter snows of January 1963, 30844 continues to get the job done near Pirbright in the soot laden snow that hung around for weeks in the great freeze.
Strathwood Library Collection

Opposite: Maunsell front end comparisons in the Windsor lines side at Clapham Junction during August 1962 between 31909 one of Maunsell's 3-cylinder Class U1 locomotives and the 2-cylinder Class S15 30839. Both exhibit overhead warning flashes on their smoke deflectors, rarities for these.
Colour Rail

Now paired to the Urie eight-wheel tender from 30499 having given up her previous six-wheel tender just before Christmas the previous year, 30835 has a clear road near Micheldever on 14 May 1964. *D.M.C. Hepburn-Scott/Rail Archive Stephenson*

Another view of 30833 with her ex-Schools Class replacement tender on shed at Eastleigh during 1963, she would take it with her to Buttigieg's scrapyard in Newport after withdrawal on 23 May 1965. Likewise, 30842 here on shed at Feltham on 26 July 1964 would take hers instead with her to Cashmore's also in Newport in 1965.
Both: Strathwood Library Collection

Having been overlooked and taken for granted as freight engines power classified as 6F they would come into demand for use in some of the many enthusiast steam specials to be run in their final years. On 18 October 1964, a spruced up 30839 clears her cylinders soon after coming off the Sturt Lane East Curve while running as part of the Midhurst Belle. Once again Feltham has cleaned up 30837 to work the Wessex Downsman on Sunday 2 May 1965, thereby drawing a few other enthusiasts lineside at Earley. **Photos: Gerald T. Robinson & The Bluebell Museum Archive**

Feltham shed would finally be forced to give up its association with both Urie and Maunsell S15s. Although 30824 had been transferred away to Eastleigh previously in June she came home to die being withdrawn officially on 5 September 1965, the day this shot was taken. Also withdrawn a fortnight later was 30837, however she was kept back and specially prepared for her starring roles with the final two rail tours run on the 9th and 16th January 1966. She looks a treat here at Eastleigh on the first tour. **Photos: Strathwood Library Collection & Rail Photoprints**

More 4-6-0s on the Southern

Opposite: In what would be its last twelve months in service the former GWR Star Class 4043 Prince Henry makes an appearance at Salisbury on a Portsmouth to Cardiff working in 1951. Built at Swindon in 1913 and now superseded by more modern 4-6-0s such as Halls, Granges, Castles and Counties who would be regulars at this spot for the next decade, until such duties became the forte of Hymeks and Swindon built DMUs next. *John Sansom*

Penetrating further into Southern Region territory was the 1935 built 5952 Cogan Hall making it to Bournemouth shed on 15 June 1952. At this time, the 81C Southall allocated locomotive was still wearing a lined black livery, as insisted upon by the authorities for mixed-traffic engines. Once again not so unusual to see an ex-GWR Hall or a Grange here either with cross-country workings during the summer timetable. ***Rail Photoprints***

Opposite: This might have been a cop for this young spotter at Waterloo on 23 May 1953, as this Standard Class 5MT had just been transferred to 70A Nine Elms from 15C Leicester Midland which had been its first shed since going into service two years beforehand.
R.C. Riley/The Transport Treasury

Another Midlands based 4-6-0 to pass through Waterloo at this time was this 3E Monument Lane based Black Five, drafted in along with several Gresley Class V2s to assist with a motive power shortage caused by some technical issues with the region's own Bulleid Pacific fleet.
R.C. Riley/The Transport Treasury

Opposite: Meanwhile the Eastern Region's 30A Stratford loaned Thompson Class B1 61329 during the late spring and early summer of 1953 to 73A Stewarts Lane. Here we see her going well through Herne Hill on 22 September after she was officially back in East London. It would not be out of the question for other class members to be seen at Brighton, Littlehampton or Eastbourne having arrived with holiday makers specials during many such summers in the fifties.
R.C. Riley/The Transport Treasury

Although she would always be a Southern Region allocated locomotive, the full blessing of her naming as Pendragon was still to be applied when seen at Stewarts Lane on 11 February 1956. In fact, the original bearer of the name 30736 had only just been taken out of service three months previously.
The Transport Treasury

Opposite: A return to Bournemouth Central on 19 August 1956 to observe another visiting ex-GWR 4-6-0 6858 Woolston Grange from Plymouth Laira running light having found its way to the Dorset coastal resort on another cross-country duty. *R.C.T.S. Archive*

It would likely have been another cross-country extra working that has brought this 15D Bedford allocated Standard Class 4MT 75042 here to the Windsor side at Clapham Junction around 1956 or 1957 as the fireman changes his lamps. *Rail Online*

Bognor Regis was another south-coast resort to host interesting visiting locomotives such as 61249 Fitzherbert Wright from 30A Stratford's allocation on 30 August 1958. The Class B1 having worked here on a service that departed from Walthamstow Wood Street at 08.20am to allow most of the day at the seaside before the journey home in the evening. *Bluebell Museum Archive*

It appears that the fireman might be digging into the lower reaches of the tender for their journey back to London on board 73082, as yet to be named Camelot from the now withdrawn King Arthur Class 30742 around 1957. *Strathwood Library Collection*

Left: This Standard Class 5MT spent its earlier days roaming around North Wales and the North West having been based at both Chester and Holyhead. However, having just arrived she would now become a Southern regular until being withdrawn just short of twelve years of service in June 1965 with her last week's being based at 70C Guildford. As a new arrival to 70A Nine Elms she caught our cameraman's attention at Victoria on 13 May 1959.
Terry Gough/The Transport Library

Opposite: The story for Standard 4MT 75068 is that she was always a Southern Region engine, although she did find herself based across all three sections at one time or another in her also sadly brief career. On 12 June 1959 she was to be seen at Cannon Street on duty.
Colour Rail

Another Standard Class 5MT to inherit a former Class N15 Arthurian legend name would be 73084 as Tintagel from the former 30745. On 13 September 1959 she had charge of Victoria to Folkstone Harbour boat train when seen passing through Sevenoaks, her name as Tintagel would be made on 7 November the same year. *Bluebell Railway Museum*

Opposite: A return to Salisbury during 1960 finds a filthy looking 1028 County of Warwick put to work today with a Portsmouth to Bristol Temple Meads service. Judging from the plentiful coal supply in her tender she has just been put on here having been serviced at the nearby Southern Region shed on behalf of Bath Road. *Neil Austin*

Opposite: In May 1962 Castle Class, 5082 Swordfish was making her way back towards the Western Region with a northbound inter-regional express at Basingstoke and would head towards Reading upon leaving the station. Notice the Great Western Hotel in the background. *Rail Photoprints*

Buffered up to another Western Region interloper resting at Eastleigh shed on 28 July 1962 was 1017 County Hereford, somewhat offbeat from her present 89A Shrewsbury home, a fill of coal with be wise before leaving. *Anistr.Com*

A further Western invader in the shape of 7910 Hown Hall has arrived deeper into Southern Region metals as far as Portsmouth Harbour, having brought in an excursion from Acton Main Line on 5 August 1962 to connect with a ferry across the Solent to the Isle of Wight. *Gerald T. Robinson*

Opposite: The Reading to Redhill route was also a regular haunt to Western Region 4-6-0s in the shape of Hawksworth designed Manor Class locomotives such as 81D Reading's 7813 Freshford Manor setting off from Betchworth in January 1963. *Tony Butcher*

Opposite: The Central Section shed at Redhill plays host to 7808 Cookham Manor on 2 March 1963 as she nestles up to Maunsell N Class Moguls 31872 and 31868, having worked in from Reading earlier in the morning. *Gerald T. Robinson*

Being one of many places where the Southern Region met every day Western Region services, Salisbury was no stranger to the likes of this Modified Hall 7922 Salford Hall in May 1963 from 81C Southall as staff go about their business. *Rail Photoprints*

The footplateman aboard Southern based Class 4MT 75070 gives us a wave as they arrive at Betchworth with another Reading to Redhill line service. Two strangers in the camp at Eastleigh as London Midland Region based Jubilee 45567 *South Australia* pushes the boundaries along with yet another Western Region 4-6-0. *Both: Strathwood Library Collection*

Freight traffic off the Western Region bound for the Southern Region brought many 4-6-0s here to Salisbury such as 88L Cardiff East Dock allocated 6957 Norcliffe Hall with the 04.17am goods from Cardiff on 8 June 1963. *Gerald T. Robinson*

Two more Western Region 4-6-0s on Southern metals with 7817 Garsington Manor at Guildford with the 12.37pm Reading service on 19 July 1963. Then three days later with 4093 Dunster Castle from 82B Bristol St. Phillips Marsh backing out light engine at Weymouth. The Dorset port being no stranger to Western engines as the shed was originally built by the GWR. **Photos: *Rail Online & Rail Photoprints***

Hampshire 4-6-0s with firstly 6841 Marlas Grange near Winchester with a Portsmouth bound inter-regional in 1964, and the now named 73082 Camelot on shed at Eastleigh the same year.
Photos: Gerald T. Robinson & Colour Rail

Just checking to see all is as it should be hauling withdrawn 6-Pan EMU stock bound for Micheldever 73171 departs Wimbledon in 1966. *Colour Rail*

Two local schoolgirls look on in September 1964 as the once briefly named Standard Class 5MT, 73081 Excalibur charges through Raynes Park having now lost those specially cast nameplates in the style of the originals once fitted to the Urie designed King Arthur 30736. *Colour Rail*

Opposite: Borrowed perhaps for this parcels working from Waterloo on 24 April 1965 was this 1E Bletchley based Black Five having most likely strayed onto the Southern Region with a cross-London goods off the London Midland Region. *Ian Turnbull/Rail Photoprints*

Ready for work the crew of double-chimney fitted Class 4MT 75077 take it easy in the sunshine as they await their next duty from Basingstoke on 24 July 1965. Whereas this Caprotti fitted Class 5MT 73133 from 9H Patricroft is both far from home nor ready for traffic carrying a leak in her tender and missing her smokebox numberplate at Eastleigh on 11 September 1965, instead she awaits a visit to the works. *Both: Strathwood Library Collection*

Finally, one of the very last 4-6-0s to work on the Southern Region would be this filthy lined green liveried Class 5MT 73092 eking out time at Basingstoke on 20 May 1967. *Gerald T. Robinson*